When Thoughts Won't Let Go

Understanding OCD with Compassion

Dave Njogu

A Babazuri Creative Firm publication

AF715368

While every precaution has been taken in the preparation of this book, the publisher assumes no responsibility for errors or omissions, or for damages resulting from the use of the information contained herein.

WHEN THOUGHTS WON'T LET GO: UNDERSTANDING OCD WITH COMPASSION

First edition. July 31, 2025.

Copyright © 2025 Dave Njogu.

ISBN: 979-8231663477

Written by Dave Njogu.

Table of Contents

Dedication

To everyone silently battling the noise in their minds—the students, the seekers, the believers, the doubters.To those who have felt afraid of their own thoughts, and to those who've been misunderstood, shamed, or dismissed—this book is for you.

And to the courageous ones who continue to show up each day despite the struggle—you are seen, you are not alone, and healing is possible.

Introduction: When the Mind Won't Keep Quiet

"I've been dealing with OCD since high school..."

It often starts silently—like a whisper in the mind, subtle and strange. You don't know what it is at first. You just know something feels *off*. For me, it began in high school.

Some church songs—especially those sung in Pentecostal churches—would trigger something deep inside me. While hymns and most choir songs were peaceful, certain lyrics with even the slightest suggestion of sensuality would disturb me. The words weren't wrong or sinful, yet something inside me reacted with overwhelming discomfort. I would begin to experience thoughts I didn't want—thoughts I couldn't shake off—until the song ended.

Other types of music affected me too—particularly secular songs in local languages. The artist may not have intended anything inappropriate, but my mind twisted the lyrics, giving them a sexual spin that was never there. That unintended twist would become a trigger. I'd struggle through the song, my thoughts racing, my spirit uneasy.

Later, the triggers spread. Religious images or drawings, though innocent and often beautiful, would unsettle me. Intrusive thoughts would push their way into my mind—uninvited and unrelenting. I tried to ignore them. I prayed harder. I wrestled silently.

The thoughts didn't stop there. They began to touch on subjects I never wanted to think about. I started having intrusive thoughts related to homosexuality—thoughts that clashed sharply with my beliefs and left me feeling ashamed and confused. I didn't choose them. I didn't want them. But they came anyway, again and again. I'm obviously straight, and I don't struggle with my orientation. What bothered me most was my strong inner reaction to homosexuality, as practiced by others. The fact that I had such thoughts at all deeply disturbed me—even when they didn't reflect who I am or what I believe. There were also other types of intrusive sexual thoughts—very different from normal desires—that deeply troubled my mind. I hesitate to describe them further, fearing they might stir up the very torment I've fought so hard to quiet.

At one point, even numbers took on a strange significance. I became obsessed with 3, 7, and 12—numbers often tied to spiritual meaning. I would try to group things in fives or twelves in my diary, feeling like there was some sacred pattern I had to follow. But it wasn't meaningful; it was exhausting. Imagine trying to organize your thoughts or your words by force—like cramming peace into a mathematical formula.

And then there was prayer. What used to be my lifeline to God slowly turned into a mental trap. I'd find myself repeating morning prayers out of fear—fear that something bad might happen if I didn't get the words exactly right. Before boarding a vehicle, I'd pray over and over again, terrified that skipping a prayer might lead to an accident. I still believe in prayer. I still value it. But when it became more about avoiding punishment than connecting with God, I knew something wasn't right.

All I wanted was peace.

All I wanted was clarity.

But my mind wouldn't let me rest.

Why This Story Matters

MANY PEOPLE THINK OF Obsessive-Compulsive Disorder (OCD) as something obvious: repeated handwashing, constant cleaning, organizing things by color or size. And yes, that is one face of OCD—but it is only one.

There is another face of OCD. A hidden one. A version that takes place entirely inside the mind, where no one else can see it.

People suffering from this type of OCD may look "fine" on the outside. They go to school. They go to work. They smile. But inside, they are waging a war against a flood of thoughts they didn't ask for—and don't want.

This book was born out of a desire to speak honestly about that struggle. To name it. To bring it into the light. And to say: **You are not alone.**

The Purpose of This Book

WHETHER YOU'RE SOMEONE experiencing OCD, a concerned parent, a pastor, a teacher, or a friend—this book is for you.

1. To Explain OCD Clearly

WE WILL UNPACK WHAT OCD is and isn't, especially the forms that are less talked about: intrusive thoughts, religious obsessions, unwanted sexual ideas, and mental rituals. You will learn that OCD is not a weakness, sin, or moral failure—but a real, diagnosable condition that affects the brain.

2. To Offer Comfort to the Silent Sufferers

MANY PEOPLE LIVING with OCD feel intense shame, thinking they are "crazy," "evil," or "unworthy." They may hide their symptoms for years. This book seeks to break the silence and offer words of compassion. If you've ever prayed over and over, avoided church music, feared your own thoughts, or felt trapped inside your mind—this is for you.

3. To Help Loved Ones Understand

OCD CAN BE CONFUSING to outsiders. It might not "make sense." The rituals might seem odd. The thoughts might seem disturbing. But behind the behavior is a person in pain. This book will help friends, spouses, siblings, and leaders respond not with judgment—but with empathy and wisdom.

This is not a medical textbook. It's a conversation. It's a guide. It's a voice saying,

"You're not broken. You're not your thoughts. And help is possible."

As we begin this journey together, I invite you to read with openness, compassion, and courage.

Let's start by understanding what OCD truly is.

Chapter 1: What Is OCD, Really?

Understanding Obsessive-Compulsive Disorder

Obsessive-Compulsive Disorder, commonly known as OCD, is a mental health condition marked by a pattern of unwanted thoughts (*obsessions*) and repetitive behaviors (*compulsions*). These obsessions and compulsions can significantly interfere with a person's daily life, relationships, and sense of peace.

OCD isn't about being tidy or liking things orderly. It's about feeling trapped in a relentless cycle of anxiety and temporary relief. The brain gets stuck on certain thoughts or fears and keeps sounding the alarm—even when there's no real danger.

Everyday Worries vs. Clinical OCD

EVERYONE HAS RANDOM worries now and then—Did I turn off the stove? Was that email okay? Did I offend someone? But in OCD, these thoughts become intrusive, repetitive, and deeply distressing. They don't go away with logic or reassurance. In fact, trying to control or avoid them often makes them stronger.

For someone with OCD, a passing doubt can spiral into hours of rumination, rituals, or fear. It's not just a personality quirk or overthinking. It's a mental health condition that affects how the brain processes uncertainty, fear, and responsibility.

Common Misconceptions

ONE OF THE BIGGEST myths about OCD is that it's all about hygiene or perfectionism. While some people with OCD may focus on cleanliness or symmetry, many others suffer from invisible battles—obsessions about morality, harm, sexuality, health, or religion.

This is why many people with OCD go undiagnosed for years. Their pain is hidden in their minds. They may seem calm on the outside while internally battling thoughts they never asked for and don't agree with.

Another harmful misconception is that people with OCD can simply "stop" their thoughts or "calm down." If they could, they would. OCD is not a choice—it's a medical condition that distorts how the mind reacts to certain thoughts or situations.

Obsessions vs. Compulsions

TO UNDERSTAND OCD, it's helpful to break it into two parts:

- **Obsessions** are intrusive thoughts, images, or urges that cause distress. These thoughts are unwanted and often go directly against a person's values or beliefs.
  Examples: "What if I committed a sin I didn't notice?" "What if I'm secretly evil?" "What if I'm attracted to something I hate?"
- **Compulsions** are the mental or physical actions a person does to try to reduce the anxiety caused by those thoughts.
  Examples: silently repeating a prayer, avoiding certain songs or images, mentally checking if a thought was sinful.

Many people think compulsions always involve visible behaviors like handwashing. But in many cases—especially with religious or sexual OCD—the compulsions happen entirely in the mind.

Together, these two parts form a loop:

Obsession → Anxiety → Compulsion → Temporary Relief → Obsession again

It becomes a cycle that's difficult to break without support or treatment.

The Impact on Thinking, Behavior, and Peace of Mind

OCD DOESN'T JUST AFFECT how you think—it affects how you live. It hijacks your time, drains your energy, and replaces joy with anxiety.

What used to be simple—praying, listening to music, boarding a vehicle, sitting in church—can become sources of overwhelming distress. The brain begins to associate peace with certainty, and when certainty isn't possible, the mind spins into overdrive trying to "solve" what can't be solved.

This creates a life of constant mental checking, avoidance, and fear.

But here's what's true:

- OCD is not a sign of weak faith.
- It's not rebellion.
- And it's not the same as sin or doubt.

It's a condition of the mind—one that millions of people quietly struggle with. But it's also treatable, and there is hope.

Coming Up Next

IN THE NEXT CHAPTER, we'll explore the wide variety of OCD subtypes—some familiar, some rarely spoken about—so you can better understand how differently OCD can show up in people's lives.

Chapter 2: Subtypes of OCD – It's More Than Just Washing Hands

A Quiet Battle Behind My Smile

I remember walking into church service, surrounded by music, warmth, and familiar faces. But inside, I was in a mental tug-of-war. As the preacher spoke of forgiveness and grace, my mind was flooded with intrusive thoughts I couldn't control—dark images, questions about whether I had sinned, urges I didn't understand. They were disturbing, unwanted, and relentless.

I would pray silently: "God, why would I think this? I don't want to... I don't mean to..." I would shake my head, as if trying to let go off me the thoughts literally!

That was one of many Sundays and Saturdays where I appeared calm on the outside while internally screaming. The guilt, shame, and fear were unbearable. I didn't dare tell anyone—who would believe me? Would they think I was dangerous? Perverted? Unholy?

This is the reality for many people with OCD. It's not always about washing hands or checking locks. *Sometimes, it's the quietest people, the kindest ones, who are silently drowning in unwanted thoughts that go against everything they believe in.*

This chapter is for those who think they're alone. You're not. And there's a name for what you're going through.

For me, the moment I discovered that what I was going through had a name—that it was known, studied, and documented—was the moment healing began. Realizing I wasn't alone made all the difference. It's heartbreaking that it took me over a decade to learn about OCD, to understand that it's a recognized mental health condition˙and that countless others face the same invisible struggle. But now, I finally feel a sense of relief—like a heavy burden has been lifted

OCD Comes in Many Forms

OCD IS NOT A ONE-SIZE-fits-all disorder. It wears many faces—some familiar, many hidden. Understanding the different subtypes helps shed light on how OCD uniquely impacts individuals. These aren't simply "preferences" or "quirks." They're distressing patterns of thought and behavior that interfere with life and peace of mind.

Let's explore the major subtypes:

1. Contamination OCD

WHAT IT FEELS LIKE:

A constant fear of germs, dirt, viruses, or chemicals. You might feel "unclean" even after showering or washing.

Compulsions include:

- Excessive handwashing or cleaning
- Avoiding public places, people, or objects
- Repeatedly changing clothes or showering

This type is the most commonly recognized, especially after the COVID-19 pandemic, but it's only one part of the picture.

2. Checking OCD

WHAT IT FEELS LIKE:

An overwhelming fear that you've made a mistake that could harm someone or cause disaster.

Compulsions include:

- Checking doors, stoves, windows, light switches
- Re-reading messages to make sure nothing offensive was said
- Seeking constant reassurançe that nothing went wrong

It's not about forgetfulness—it's about fear. Even after checking, your brain screams, *"But what if..."*

3. Order & Symmetry OCD

WHAT IT FEELS LIKE:

A strong urge for things to feel *just right.* As if the universe won't be okay until the items on your desk are perfectly aligned.

Compulsions include:

- Rearranging objects until they feel balanced
- Counting or tapping in even numbers
- Avoiding odd numbers or asymmetrical patterns

It's not about liking neatness—it's about relieving inner chaos.

4. Harm OCD (Aggression & Violence)

WHAT IT FEELS LIKE:

Horrifying, intrusive thoughts about harming others or yourself—even those you love the most.

Examples of thoughts:

- "What if I pushed someone in front of a car?"
- "What if I suddenly stab someone?"
- "Am I secretly a murderer?"

These thoughts are terrifying, precisely because they are the opposite of who you are. You're not dangerous—your OCD is.

5. Sexual Intrusive Thoughts OCD

WHAT IT FEELS LIKE:

Unwanted sexual thoughts that disturb and shame you. These often involve taboo or socially unacceptable themes.

Examples include:

- Thoughts about inappropriate sexual behavior
- Worries about being a pedophile, even without attraction
- Doubting your sexual orientation repeatedly

These are not fantasies. They're intrusive, unwelcome, and cause extreme mental suffering.

6. Scrupulosity (Religious/Moral OCD)

WHAT IT FEELS LIKE:

Obsessions about sin, morality, or spiritual worthiness. You might feel like you've blasphemed or offended God—even when you haven't.

Compulsions include:

- Repetitive praying or confessing
- Avoiding "sinful" songs, movies, or images
- Constantly checking your motives or thoughts for hidden evil

This subtype is especially tormenting for the religious. It twists faith into fear.

7. Relationship OCD

WHAT IT FEELS LIKE:

Doubts and intrusive thoughts about your romantic relationship—even when nothing is wrong.

Examples include:

- "Do I really love them?"
- "What if they cheat on me?"
- "Am I attracted enough to them?"

You may seek reassurance, overanalyze every feeling, or constantly compare your relationship with others.

---

8. Health Anxiety OCD (Hypochondria OCD)

WHAT IT FEELS LIKE:

A relentless belief that you're seriously ill—even when doctors say you're fine.

Compulsions include:

- Googling symptoms obsessively
- Repeated doctor visits
- Scanning your body for signs of illness

It's more than worrying—it's being mentally hijacked by fear of dying, deteriorating, or being misdiagnosed.

Why These Subtypes Matter

EVERY PERSON WITH OCD has a unique experience. Some have one main theme; others have several that shift over time. The content of the obsessions may differ, but the pain, fear, and confusion they cause are the same.

Understanding these subtypes isn't about boxing people into categories. It's about giving language to suffering—so you can name what's happening, seek help, and begin healing.

If any of these descriptions made your heart race or brought tears to your eyes, please know this:

You are not alone.

You are not dangerous.

You are not your thoughts.

You are worthy of compassion, healing, and peace.

Chapter 3: The Hidden Face – Taboo OCD Themes

"*The thoughts are not who you are. The fear is not a reflection of your heart.*"

When most people hear the word OCD, they picture someone who is overly neat, obsessed with handwashing or organizing their shoes. But for many of us living with OCD, the most painful parts are not visible. They live silently inside the mind — deeply disturbing, confusing, and unwanted thoughts that attack the very core of who we are. These are what some therapists call **"taboo OCD themes."**

They are not just about being tidy or cautious. They revolve around topics so unsettling that many sufferers hide in shame for years, unable to speak. These include intrusive thoughts about violence, sex, religion, and health — not because we want to think them, but precisely because we **don't**.

Let's gently explore these themes, not to shock, but to give language to the invisible pain many carry alone — and to say: *You are not your thoughts. You are not alone.*

---

1. Aggression & Violence OCD

"WHAT IF I LOSE CONTROL and harm someone I love?"

This form of OCD is rooted in a terrifying fear: the fear that you might hurt others or yourself, even though you don't want to. These are not impulses or desires. They are **intrusive thoughts** that come **against** your values and identity, which is what makes them so distressing.

Examples include:

- A sudden mental image of stabbing a loved one while holding a kitchen knife.
- A fear that you might push someone into traffic.
- Worry that you could blurt out something violent or abusive to a child or elderly person.

Common compulsions:

- Avoiding sharp objects or kitchen tools.
- Seeking reassurance: "You'd tell me if I ever hurt anyone, right?"
- Replaying the thought to prove you wouldn't do it.

This might be you:

Walking near balconies or rooftops, afraid you'd push someone off — not because you want to, but because you feared what your mind showed you. You felt like a hidden danger, a monster — until you now learned it was just OCD.

---

2. Scrupulosity (Religious and Moral OCD)

"WHAT IF I BLASPHEME, sin, or offend God without realizing?"

For religious people, faith is sacred. But OCD can weaponize that very devotion and turn it into an endless loop of guilt, fear, and internal punishment. Scrupulosity is a type of OCD that attaches to religious or moral ideas and creates extreme fear of being sinful, immoral, or spiritually unworthy.

Signs of Scrupulosity:

- Fear of going to hell over a "bad" thought.
- Repeating prayers perfectly or multiple times to "make them

count."

- Avoiding religious activities for fear of doing them wrong.
- Obsessive confession — sometimes even for thoughts, not actions.

Examples:

- A Muslim afraid they didn't perform wudhu (ablution) "properly" and repeats it again and again.
- A Christian who fears they accidentally cursed God in their mind and fears eternal damnation.
- A believer who avoids reading sacred texts for fear of misinterpreting or disrespecting them.

Compulsion isn't faith. It's fear wearing the mask of devotion.

---

3. Sexual Obsessions

"WHY AM I HAVING THESE disturbing thoughts? Does this mean I'm evil or perverted?"

This is one of the hardest forms of OCD to talk about. It hijacks one of the most personal parts of our humanity — sexuality — and distorts it into fearful, unwanted thoughts. These are **not fantasies or desires**, but rather intrusive thoughts that horrify the person experiencing them.

Examples:

- A straight man having unwanted sexual thoughts about other men and fearing he might be secretly gay.
- A woman who fears she might be sexually attracted to children, even though she finds the thought revolting.
- Thoughts involving religious figures, animals, or family members.

The reaction is always the same: shame, self-disgust, and panic. Many sufferers avoid intimacy, children, or even their own partners, fearing they might act on these thoughts.

But here's the truth:

The very fact that these thoughts cause **distress** proves they are **not aligned** with who you are. OCD latches onto what you value most — your morality, your faith, your love for others — and creates fear around losing or violating it.

---

4. Health-Related OCD

"WHAT IF I HAVE A DISEASE no doctor can find?"

This form of OCD is often mistaken for general health anxiety, but it's more intense, persistent, and driven by compulsive behavior. It includes obsessive fear of illness, contamination, or hidden infections.

Examples:

- Repeated doctor visits even after getting clean bills of health.
- Googling symptoms multiple times a day.
- Constant body scanning: checking your pulse, lumps, sensations, or irregularities.
- Avoiding hospitals or touching public surfaces due to fear of illness.

Health OCD is not about being cautious. It's about a mind that won't stop shouting "what if?" even when logic and evidence say otherwise.

This might be you:

YOU spent months convinced YOU had an undiagnosed illness. YOU Googled symptoms so much that your browser history looked like a medical textbook.YouI didn't want attention — YOU just wanted peace of mind.

Final Thoughts

OCD IS OFTEN DESCRIBED as "the doubting disease." Nowhere is that more painful than with taboo themes. These thoughts are intrusive, unwanted, and feel like betrayals of the very person you are. But they are not. They are symptoms — not signs of who you are or what you will do.

Chapter 4: What OCD Might Look Like – Everyday Examples

OCD doesn't always wear a dramatic face. Many people suffer silently with patterns that appear subtle to others but are deeply exhausting and disruptive. These are a few common real-life examples that reveal how OCD can quietly seep into everyday life:

1. Repeating Prayers "Just Right" Before Leaving the House

YOU'RE PREPARING TO leave home, but something feels off. A short prayer turns into a long, mentally exhausting ritual. You repeat the words several times, each time trying to get the tone, emotion, or phrase *exactly right*—believing that unless it's perfect, harm may come to you or your loved ones. Even when running late, you can't leave until it feels "done right."

2. Feeling Anxious If Items Aren't Symmetrical or Aligned

IMAGINE SITTING IN your living room and noticing that a cushion is slightly tilted. Your brain won't let it go. You stand, fix it, sit, look again—and repeat the process several times until everything feels "even." It's not about aesthetics. It's an inner tension, like a mental itch that won't fade until the order feels perfect.

3. Avoiding Religious Gatherings for Fear of Intrusive Thoughts

A PLACE THAT ONCE GAVE you peace now triggers dread. You avoid church or mosque not because of disbelief, but because your mind might bombard you with unwanted, distressing thoughts—blasphemy, guilt, or even perverse ideas. You fear you'll offend God just by showing up with such thoughts in your head.

4. Canceling Trips or Work Because of a "Bad Number"

YOU'RE INVITED FOR a trip or an important work event. But the date has a number that feels "wrong" or "unlucky." Maybe it's the 6th, or 13th, or something personal like a time of day. Logic tells you it's silly, but anxiety wins. You cancel. Later, you feel relieved... but also controlled.

5. Constant Mental Review: "Did I Sin?" "Did I Blaspheme?"

YOU REPLAY YOUR WORDS and thoughts from hours ago. Did you speak with pride? Did a joke cross the line? Was that thought during prayer a sin? The questions loop endlessly. Even after confessing or apologizing, your mind won't let go. You doubt your own sincerity and moral worth.

6. Seeking Reassurance from Friends or Religious Leaders

YOU REGULARLY ASK PEOPLE questions like:

"Is it sinful if I thought this?"

"Do you think I offended God?"

"Is this a normal thought?"

You trust their answers briefly... then ask again later, or ask someone else. The relief is short-lived. You start to feel guilty for bothering people, yet can't stop seeking reassurance.

Final Thought for the Reader

THESE EXAMPLES MIGHT seem mild on the surface, but for someone living with OCD, they can be mentally exhausting and emotionally paralyzing. The compulsions are not "quirks" or mere habits—they are attempts to soothe unbearable anxiety caused by obsessive thoughts.

If these stories feel uncomfortably familiar, you're not alone. You're not broken. And you're not guilty. OCD is not a character flaw—it's a mental condition that can be managed with support, therapy, and understanding.

Chapter 5: Where Do These Thoughts Come From?

One of the most unsettling things about living with OCD is the nature of the thoughts themselves—how sudden, bizarre, disturbing, and completely out of character they can be. Many people ask, *"Why would I even think that?"* or *"What does it say about me?"* The shame can be crushing, and the confusion overwhelming. But to begin finding clarity and compassion for oneself, it helps to understand where these thoughts come from—and why they feel so powerful.

The Brain Science Behind OCD

OCD IS NOT A CHARACTER flaw or a result of weak faith or morality. It's rooted in brain circuitry. Research using brain imaging has shown that individuals with OCD have increased activity in certain areas of the brain—especially the **orbitofrontal cortex**, **anterior cingulate cortex**, and **basal ganglia**. These regions are involved in decision-making, error detection, and habit formation. For someone with OCD, this system goes into overdrive.

Imagine a "warning system" that keeps going off, even when there's no real danger. The brain says, *"Something's wrong, fix it,"* but it can't quite explain what or why. So the mind starts scanning for potential dangers—and intrusive thoughts begin to form.

Why Logical Thinking Doesn't Always Work

MANY PEOPLE WITH OCD are intelligent, insightful, and capable of reasoning. So it's frustrating when logic seems powerless. You might *know* your thought isn't realistic—yet the emotional part of your brain doesn't believe it.

For example, you might know you're not going to harm your loved one, but the *feeling* of danger remains. This is because OCD bypasses logic and attaches fear directly to thoughts, regardless of their content. Trying to argue with it is like trying to reason with a smoke alarm during a fire drill—it's wired to make noise, not to think.

Why Intrusive Thoughts Feel So Personal

OCD IS OFTEN CALLED the "doubting disorder," but more than that, it hijacks what you care about most. The content of intrusive thoughts often targets your **core values**. A kind, gentle person may obsess over violent images. A devoted person of faith may be bombarded with blasphemous ideas. A loving parent may be haunted by fears of harming their child.

These thoughts are not a reflection of your character—they're the opposite. Their power lies in how deeply they contradict who you are. And that's why they hurt so much.

The Guilt Loop

HERE'S WHAT OFTEN HAPPENS in the mind of someone with OCD:

1. **Intrusive Thought**: A sudden, unwanted idea or image appears (e.g., *"What if I cursed God?"*)
2. **Guilt and Anxiety**: You feel shame, fear, or moral panic—*"What if I've sinned?"*

3. **Compulsion**: You perform a mental or physical ritual to feel safe again—perhaps repeating a prayer or seeking reassurance.
4. **Temporary Relief**: For a brief moment, the fear subsides.
5. **Repeat**: Soon, the thought returns—and the cycle begins again.

This loop can dominate a person's life, draining energy, joy, and time. It's exhausting, but it's not hopeless. Understanding that this is a pattern—not a moral failure—is the first step to breaking free.

Chapter 6: Treatment and Relief – There Is Hope

After years of confusion, shame, and silence, discovering that there is effective treatment for OCD can feel like someone finally turning on the light in a dark room. OCD may be powerful, but it's not untouchable. With the right support, knowledge, and tools, healing is possible—and very real.

This chapter introduces the most effective, research-backed ways people manage and reduce OCD symptoms. The good news is: **OCD is treatable**, and many people have gone on to live full and meaningful lives.

---

1. Cognitive Behavioral Therapy (CBT)

THE GOLD STANDARD OF OCD Treatment

Cognitive Behavioral Therapy is a structured, goal-oriented therapy that helps people understand how their thoughts, feelings, and behaviors are connected. For OCD, the most effective form is a special type of CBT called **Exposure and Response Prevention (ERP)**.

How ERP Works:

- **Exposure** means gradually facing the intrusive thought or feared situation—without trying to neutralize it.
- **Response Prevention** means **resisting the compulsion** (such as washing, checking, or seeking reassurance) even though it

feels uncomfortable.

THIS MIGHT SOUND SCARY at first, but ERP is done **gently and with guidance**, often starting with mild exposures and working up gradually. Over time, the brain learns that the fear **doesn't need to control your life**, and the anxiety begins to fade.

Many people describe ERP as "retraining the brain to stop reacting like there's danger when there isn't."

"Before ERP, my OCD controlled my every decision. Now, I feel like I have a choice."

---

2. Medication

WHEN THE BRAIN NEEDS a Little Help

Medication isn't a magic pill—but for many, it's a game-changer.

The most commonly used medications for OCD are **Selective Serotonin Reuptake Inhibitors (SSRIs)**. These include:

- **Fluoxetine** (Prozac)
- **Sertraline** (Zoloft)
- **Fluvoxamine**
- **Paroxetine** (Paxil)
- **Escitalopram** (Lexapro)

How They Help:

THESE MEDICATIONS **adjust the levels of serotonin in the brain**, which helps reduce the intensity and frequency of obsessions and compulsions. They often take 4–8 weeks to show noticeable results.

In many cases, **medication works best when combined with CBT**.

You don't need to take them forever. Some people use medication short-term to reduce the "noise" of OCD enough to fully engage in therapy. Others stay on it longer as part of their long-term care. There's no one-size-fits-all plan—only what works best for you.

---

3. Mindfulness and Acceptance

ANOTHER WAY TO DEAL with the Storm

Not everyone responds well to traditional methods alone. That's where practices like **Mindfulness** and **Acceptance and Commitment Therapy (ACT)** can help.

The Core Idea:

RATHER THAN FIGHTING or avoiding intrusive thoughts, you learn to **notice them** without reacting. This can break the cycle of fear and compulsion.

- You learn that a thought is **just a thought**, not a prophecy or a truth.
- You practice **"sitting with the discomfort"** rather than rushing to make it go away.

This can be life-changing for people whose OCD is filled with guilt, shame, or fear of what their thoughts "mean" about them.

Example:

INSTEAD OF THINKING, *"Why did I have that horrible thought? Does it mean I'm evil?"*, a mindfulness approach teaches you to say:

"There's that thought again. It's uncomfortable, but I don't have to do anything about it."

Over time, the thought loses its power.

---

4. Faith-Friendly Approaches

HEALING THAT HONORS **Your Beliefs**

For people struggling with **scrupulosity**—the OCD that targets your faith, morality, or sense of spiritual purity—it's vital to know this:

You don't have to choose between healing and your faith.

Faith-sensitive therapists **respect your religious values** and work with you to separate your true beliefs from OCD's distortions.

What Faith-Aware Therapy Looks Like:

- Using **scripture and prayer** as sources of strength—not as tools for compulsion.
- Understanding the **difference between sin and OCD guilt**.
- Collaborating with your religious leaders when helpful.
- Helping you rediscover joy in your spiritual life, without fear.

MANY PEOPLE FIND THAT as their OCD gets better, their relationship with God also becomes **more peaceful, more loving, and less fear-based**.

A Personal Word:

HEALING MAY TAKE TIME. Progress might be slow. Some days will be easier than others. But there is **real hope**. You are not broken. You are not alone. And you are not beyond healing.

OCD is not a result of weak faith or poor character. It is a condition that can be managed with compassion, science, and courage.

And yes—**you deserve peace.**

Chapter 7: The Hidden Strengths of OCD Minds

OCD is often framed in terms of its challenges—and understandably so. The constant noise, the fear, the rituals, and the guilt can make everyday life feel like an unending uphill climb. But that is not the whole story. Beneath the struggle lies something surprisingly beautiful: a mind wired for care, depth, and complexity. People with OCD often possess hidden strengths that, when recognized and nurtured, can become profound assets to themselves and the world around them.

1. High Attention to Detail

MANY INDIVIDUALS WITH OCD naturally pay close attention to things others overlook. This attentiveness can be exhausting when focused on perceived threats or imperfections. However, it also means that someone with OCD may excel in roles that require precision—like editing, designing, coding, writing, quality control, research, or even art.

The same mind that notices a slightly crooked picture frame or a missed word in a document is capable of catching vital errors, refining ideas, and crafting excellence. With healing and guidance, this gift can thrive outside the grip of anxiety.

2. Deep Conscience and Moral Awareness

OCD OFTEN FIXATES ON moral and ethical questions. "Was that lie a sin?" "Did I offend someone without realizing?" While painful in the form of scrupulosity, this intense moral compass points to something noble: a sincere desire to do what is right.

Many with OCD are deeply compassionate. They're the ones who think twice before speaking, who feel others' pain deeply, who care about integrity even when no one is watching. In a world that can feel careless, this sensitivity is not a weakness—it's a light.

3. Intense Focus and Drive

WHEN NOT CLOUDED BY anxiety, the OCD mind can lock into a task with remarkable dedication. This ability to focus deeply—sometimes obsessively—can be channeled into work, study, or creative pursuits. The same person who reviews their thoughts a hundred times may also be capable of studying a topic deeply, perfecting a skill, or building a project to completion with excellence.

It's not about turning OCD into a "superpower." It's about recognizing that the mind trained to dig deep has unique potential when given healthier outlets.

4. Strong Empathy and Concern for Others

MANY PEOPLE WITH OCD are unusually empathetic. Why? Because they spend a lot of time inside their own heads, wrestling with the pain of doubt, guilt, and fear. This makes them more likely to understand the hidden battles others face.

Their empathy isn't shallow. It's informed by lived experience—the kind of compassion that doesn't rush to fix but chooses to sit with someone in their darkness. This makes them good listeners, caring friends, and gentle caregivers.

5. Creativity Through Struggle

LIVING WITH OCD OFTEN forces people to find creative ways to cope, soothe, and express themselves. Whether through journaling, drawing, music, storytelling, or problem-solving, many with OCD develop vibrant creative lives.

What's more, the internal storm they navigate gives their creativity depth. They don't create from a place of ease—they create from a place of truth. And truth connects.

Reflection:

It's easy to see OCD only as a disorder that takes. But it's also shaped minds that give—minds that reflect deeply, feel richly, and love fiercely. The journey toward healing doesn't erase these qualities—it brings them into the light.

If you live with OCD, know this: your strengths are real. They may be tangled up in struggle now, but they're waiting—quietly, patiently—to be set free and put to good use.

Let no one convince you that your value is only in your recovery. Your value has always been there, hidden like treasure beneath the noise.

Chapter 8: For Those Who Suffer – You Are Not Alone

You are not alone. You are not broken. You are not your thoughts.

Living with OCD can feel like walking through a silent storm—your heart pounding, your mind racing, all while the world moves on, unaware of the battle inside. For many, the pain is invisible, misunderstood, or dismissed. But if you're reading this, take heart: you're seen, you're not alone, and there is hope.

⚙ To the Student Battling Mental Rituals Before Class

YOU SIT IN CLASS BUT hardly hear the lesson. You're busy counting, mentally repeating a phrase, or reviewing a thought until it feels "just right." You're not lazy or distracted—you're exhausted from a mental marathon no one else can see. Your efforts are not in vain. You're showing up, even when it's hard. That's courage.

"At one point, I had to say a prayer exactly seven times before entering the classroom. If I lost count or someone distracted me, I started over. It was draining, but I thought if I didn't, something terrible would happen. Therapy helped me slowly take my life back." – Grace, 20

⟐ To the Young Person Confused About Their Intrusive Thoughts

YOU'RE SCARED, MAYBE even ashamed. The thoughts that pop into your head feel unbearable: violent, sexual, blasphemous. You ask yourself, *"Why am I thinking this? Does it mean I'm bad?"* No. These thoughts are not who you are. They are symptoms of OCD—unwanted, automatic mental noise that latch onto what you fear most.

"I thought I was going crazy. I couldn't tell anyone what was going through my head—it was too awful. But then I learned these are called intrusive thoughts, and they happen to a lot of people with OCD. Knowing that changed everything." – Sammy, 17

⟐ To the Churchgoer Who Feels Sinful or Broken

YOU AVOID CHURCH. OR when you go, your prayers feel empty because you're stuck in a cycle of doubt, fear, and guilt. You've confessed the same thing a hundred times, but it never feels resolved. You're not lacking faith. You're not possessed. You're suffering from scrupulosity—a form of OCD that attaches itself to the sacred. Healing is possible without abandoning your beliefs.

"I used to confess every thought, every doubt, terrified I had offended God. I felt unworthy to pray. When I finally found a therapist who understood faith, I began to heal. God never abandoned me—I just needed help." – Daniel, 35

☹ To the Adult Worn Out by the Mental Noise

MAYBE YOU'VE LIVED with this for years, quietly. You're good at hiding it—at work, in your marriage, with your friends. But inside, the wheels never stop spinning. You review, replay, avoid, question. You're tired. You don't have to carry this forever. Healing is not instant, but it is real.

"For a long time, I thought I was just overly cautious or perfectionistic. But it wasn't normal to spend hours checking doors or rewriting texts ten times. Therapy helped me realize I had OCD. Naming it was the first step to healing." – Miriam, 42

◈ Final Words of Comfort

OCD DOESN'T MAKE YOU weak, dangerous, or defective. It means your brain sends faulty alarms—loud, distressing, and persistent. But it is treatable. With therapy, support, and often faith-affirming care, people go on to live full, meaningful lives.

You are not your thoughts.

You are not your compulsions.

You are brave for facing each day.

And if no one has told you today: you are loved, you are worthy, and there is a path forward.

◈ Want to Talk About It?

WHETHER YOU'RE A READER silently struggling or someone seeking help for a loved one, speaking out is not a weakness—it's an act of strength. The more we talk about OCD, especially the misunderstood types, the less shame others will carry in silence.

You matter. Don't give up. Healing is possible.

Chapter 9: How Friends, Families, and Faith Leaders Can Help

Obsessive-Compulsive Disorder can feel like an invisible prison. Those suffering often appear "fine" on the outside but are battling tormenting thoughts and rituals internally. Support from loved ones and spiritual leaders can make a meaningful difference in their healing journey—but only when it's informed, compassionate, and consistent.

Understanding the Role of Support

WHEN SOMEONE OPENS up about OCD, they're not simply sharing "worries." They're revealing a vulnerable part of themselves that they may have hidden for years out of shame or fear of being misunderstood. Your response can either build a bridge or deepen their isolation.

How to Support Someone with OCD

1. Listen Without Judgment

THE MOST POWERFUL GIFT you can offer is your presence. Listen attentively—even if their fears seem irrational. Understand that OCD is not a logic problem; it's a neurological condition. When they say they're terrified they may have offended God by thinking a blasphemous thought, don't minimize it. Don't try to "fix" it. Just acknowledge it kindly.

"That must feel really heavy. I'm here with you."

This simple posture—of respect and patience—communicates safety.

2. Avoid Giving Constant Reassurance

IT MAY FEEL NATURAL to say:

- "You're fine."
- "You didn't sin."
- "You prayed correctly."
- "God knows your heart."

While well-intentioned, these reassurances can become part of the OCD cycle. The sufferer may become dependent on others to feel temporarily "okay," instead of learning how to tolerate the anxiety and let it pass.

Instead of answering compulsive questions, try:

"I know this feels upsetting, but maybe your OCD is asking that question, not you."

"What would you like to do that aligns with your recovery goals?"

This redirects them toward managing their OCD, not fueling it.

3. Learn the Difference Between Support and Enabling

SUPPORT MEANS WALKING beside someone without removing their discomfort. Enabling is doing the compulsions for them—or feeding the cycle of fear and relief. Here's the difference:

- **Support**: "I know you're anxious, but let's sit with that feeling together for a bit."
- **Enabling**: "Okay, I'll check the door lock for you—again."

Compulsions feed OCD, even when done by someone else. Loving someone with OCD sometimes means allowing them to be uncomfortable without trying to take the feeling away.

4. Encourage Professional Help Early

OCD IS TREATABLE. BUT it often goes undiagnosed for years, especially in religious communities where it is mistaken for moral failure, weak faith, or lack of prayer. If you suspect someone may be struggling:

- Recommend speaking to a licensed therapist—especially one trained in Cognitive Behavioral Therapy (CBT) or Exposure and Response Prevention (ERP).
- Help them understand that seeking help is not weakness. It's wisdom.

Faith and therapy are not in conflict. In fact, they can complement each other beautifully when approached with integrity.

Common Mistakes to Avoid

EVEN WITH THE BEST intentions, loved ones can sometimes say or do things that unintentionally make the struggle worse. Here's what to watch out for:

1. Dismissing OCD as "Just Overthinking"

TELLING SOMEONE WITH OCD to "just stop thinking about it" or "snap out of it" is not helpful. OCD is not a choice. It's not something that can be willed away with positive thinking. Comments like:

- "Everyone worries. You're being dramatic."
- "You just need to have more faith."

...may silence the person permanently. They might retreat into their own mind, thinking no one understands.

Instead, validate their struggle while guiding them toward help.

2. Using Shame or Religious Guilt

RELIGIOUS OCD (SCRUPULOSITY) can be worsened when spiritual leaders use guilt to pressure obedience or perfection. Saying things like:

- "If your faith were strong, you wouldn't feel this way."
- "Those thoughts are sinful—you must repent harder."

...may only increase the person's anxiety and internal shame.

The goal of faith should be peace and healing, not fear and punishment. Leaders can emphasize the unconditional love and mercy of God, reminding sufferers that intrusive thoughts do not define their soul.

What Real Support Looks Like

- A parent who learns about ERP to better support their child.
- A spouse who gently resists doing compulsions and encourages therapy.
- A pastor who publicly acknowledges mental health issues in sermons.
- A friend who checks in regularly, not to fix, but to walk beside.

THESE ACTS ARE NOT grand—but they are powerful.

Final Words to the Supporters

IF SOMEONE HAS TRUSTED you with their pain, honor that trust. You don't need all the answers. You just need to show up with love, patience, and the humility to learn.

Because when a person with OCD begins to believe: *"I'm not alone... Someone sees me... I'm still loved,"*—that is when true healing begins.

Chapter 10: Finding Peace One Thought at a Time

Healing from OCD—especially religious or moral OCD—rarely comes in one big, sweeping moment. It's more like learning to walk again after a long illness: small steps, often shaky, but each one counts. Progress isn't always loud or visible to others—but it's real.

This chapter offers gentle, practical tools and reminders for anyone seeking peace—not perfect peace, but real peace. The kind that grows with time and effort.

---

1. Small Daily Practices That Help

YOU DON'T NEED TO OVERHAUL your entire life in one day. Begin with small, consistent practices that calm your mind, re-center your emotions, and help retrain your responses.

• Journaling

A SAFE PLACE FOR YOUR thoughts. Write about the obsessions, the fears, the guilt—and the progress. Over time, journaling helps separate your **thoughts from your identity**. You may even begin to notice patterns that aren't as powerful as they first seemed.

Try this prompt: "What did OCD say today? What do I say back?"

• Grounding Techniques

OCD OFTEN PULLS YOUR mind far into a hypothetical future or deep into past regrets. Grounding helps bring you back to **the here and now**.

Simple grounding tools include:

- **5-4-3-2-1 Technique**: Name 5 things you can see, 4 you can touch, 3 you can hear, 2 you can smell, 1 you can taste.
- **Deep breathing**: Inhale slowly for 4 counts, hold for 4, exhale for 6.
- **Describing your surroundings aloud**: "I'm in my room. It's safe. I'm sitting. I can hear birds outside."

• Limiting Avoidance

AVOIDANCE GIVES OCD strength. It convinces your brain that something is dangerous, when it isn't.

Instead of skipping the prayer, skipping the church service, or avoiding touching a Bible—try approaching them gently. Start small. Stay for five minutes. Practice tolerance of discomfort. It's not easy—but it's healing.

• Creating Supportive Routines

STRUCTURE SOOTHES ANXIETY. When your brain knows what's coming next, it doesn't work so hard trying to predict or control everything.

Design routines that support your peace:

- A simple morning ritual (drink water, pray, stretch, write a kind thought).

- Regular sleep and eating patterns.
- Daily "quiet time" for reflection without pressure.

---

2. Knowing When to Seek Help Again

RELAPSES HAPPEN. THAT doesn't mean you've failed—it means you're human.

If you notice:

- Compulsions increasing again
- Intrusive thoughts taking over your day
- Avoidance or shame creeping back

...it might be time to reach out for extra help.

There is no shame in returning to therapy, adjusting your medication, or seeking renewed guidance. True strength is knowing when to ask.

---

3. Celebrate the Small Wins

NOT CHECKING THAT VERSE twice today? That's a win.

Going to service even when your brain screamed at you? Huge win.

Tolerating a scary thought without a compulsion? That's therapy working.

Write it down. Mark it somehow. Celebrate progress—because healing is made of thousands of quiet victories no one else sees. **But you know. And God knows.**

Final Word: Peace is Possible

PEACE DOESN'T ALWAYS mean silence. Sometimes, it means **a new way of relating to noise.**

It means recognizing:

You are not your thoughts. You are not your fears. You are the person showing up every day in spite of them.

Healing isn't a destination. It's a relationship you rebuild—with yourself, with your mind, with God.

Keep going. One thought at a time.

Appendix: Tools, Help, and Hope for the Journey Ahead

This appendix is your companion as you move forward—whether you're living with OCD, supporting someone who is, or simply want to understand more. It includes recommended resources, professional contacts, and tools you can use immediately.

1. Helpful Resources on OCD

THESE WEBSITES AND materials offer solid, science-based, and often faith-respecting information on OCD.

◈ Websites

- **International OCD Foundation (IOCDF)**[1]: A well-known source of OCD facts, treatment options, and real-life stories.
- **Made of Millions Foundation**[2]: Global mental health platform with real, raw stories and advocacy tools.
- **OCD Kenya (Facebook Group)**[3]: A growing Kenyan online support community where sufferers and supporters share experiences.
- **NOCD**[4]: Offers affordable virtual OCD therapy with licensed

1. https://iocdf.org
2. https://www.madeofmillions.com
3. https://www.facebook.com/groups/OCDKenya
4. https://www.treatmyocd.com

professionals, including ERP-focused care.

⟐ YouTube Channels

- **Ali Greymond** – Practical ERP advice from someone who's been there.
- **OCD and Anxiety Online (Nathan Peterson, therapist)** – Simple explanations and strategies for intrusive thoughts and ERP.
- **Chrissie Hodges** – Honest, vulnerable discussions about OCD and recovery.
- **The OCD Stories** – Expert interviews, survivor stories, and faith-sensitive advice.

⟐ Books to Read

- *Freedom from Obsessive-Compulsive Disorder* by Jonathan Grayson
- *The Mindfulness Workbook for OCD* by Jon Hershfield & Tom Corboy
- *God and Mental Illness* by Dr. Matthew Stanford (for Christian readers)
- *Can Christianity Cure Obsessive-Compulsive Disorder?* by Ian Osborn

---

2. Find a Therapist: Start Where You Are

WHILE GLOBAL DIRECTORIES help, we understand that access to mental health care is different in Africa. Below are some options tailored to local and regional needs.

⟐ Directories & Local Networks

- **TherapyRoute Africa**[5]: Lists psychologists and therapists across Kenya, Uganda, South Africa, and other African countries.
- **PSK – Psychological Society of Kenya**[6]: Directory of registered psychologists and counselors in Kenya.
- **Mindful Kenya**[7]: Nairobi-based group offering therapy, including for OCD and anxiety.
- **Local hospitals & universities**: Moi, Kenyatta, Nairobi, and Aga Khan University hospitals often have mental health services and trained therapists.
- **Faith-based counseling centers** (check in local churches or denominations): Many are opening up to mental health referrals and support.

---

3. Sample ERP Worksheet (Exposure and Response Prevention)

USE THIS TEMPLATE TO begin your exposure journey slowly. Do this with a therapist if possible.

5. https://www.therapyroute.com

6. https://psk.or.ke

7. https://www.mindfulkenya.org

Intrusive Thought	Feared Outcome	Avoidance/ Compulsion	Exposure Plan	Difficulty Level (1-10)	Response Prevention
I might harm someone	I will lose control	Avoiding knives	Sit near kitchen knife for 5 mins daily	7	Do not leave room, do not seek reassurance
I had a blasphemous thought	God will punish me	Excessive praying	Read scripture with blasphemous thoughts present	8	Allow thought to come, do not pray to cancel

◈ *Note: ERP is uncomfortable at first—but over time, it helps retrain the brain.*

---

4. Self-Reflection Journal Template

A DAILY OR WEEKLY JOURNAL to track thoughts, reactions, and growth. This can help you recognize patterns and progress.

◈ **Date:**

◈ **Intrusive Thought(s):**

◈ **How I Responded:**

⚖ **Was It a Compulsion or Acceptance?:**

◈ **What Helped Me Cope Today:**

◈ **Prayer/Scripture/Quote That Gave Me Strength:**

◈ **One Small Win I Can Celebrate:**

◈ **What I Want to Try Tomorrow:**

Final Note:

You may feel alone in your struggles, but help is available—and healing is possible. Whether it's ERP therapy, a supportive faith community, or journaling your truth, each step matters.

Keep showing up. Keep choosing hope.

Don't miss out!

Visit the website below and you can sign up to receive emails whenever Dave Njogu publishes a new book. There's no charge and no obligation.

https://books2read.com/r/B-A-IGXZ-CSVSG

BOOKS 2 READ

Connecting independent readers to independent writers.

Did you love *When Thoughts Won't Let Go: Understanding OCD with Compassion*? Then you should read *Becoming a Top Scorer: Lessons for Academic Excellence*[8] by Dave Njogu!

[9]

Read more at https://x.com/bcreativefirm.

8. https://books2read.com/u/md9yDE

9. https://books2read.com/u/md9yDE

Also by Dave Njogu

101 Common Questions Answered
Mastering Business English Q&A

Standalone
The Healing Harvest: Organic Farming 101
Unlock Your Authorial Potential:The Ultimate Guide to Crafting and Selling eBooks Using ChatGPT and Draft2digit
Herbs and Spices: Nature's Remedies for Health and Wellness
Grit and Growth: Unleashing Mental Toughness for Small Business Success
Design Mastery: Principles of Page Layout and Typography for Beginners
The Quantity Advantage: Achieving Excellence Through Abundance
The 17 Business Lessons: Insights from Christo Wiese
Silent Hustle - Mastering Remote Work And Digital Creation For Introverts
Non-Serial Entrepreneurship: A Guide to Building Lasting Success
Strategic Requests: How to Leverage Connections for Personal and Professional Growth
The Micro-Education Entrepreneur: Unlock Your Potential, Monetize Your Knowledge, and Thrive in the Digital Era

Discovering the Toyota Prius Hybrid: Your Easy Guide to Eco-Friendly Driving
Discovering Toyota Rav4 Hybrid: Your Easy Guide to Eco-Friendly Driving
Frame It Right: A Step-by-Step Guide to Starting Your Photo Mounting Business
Becoming a Top Scorer: Lessons for Academic Excellence
Creative Freedom: the World of Free & Open-Source Creative Suite
When Thoughts Won't Let Go: Understanding OCD with Compassion

Watch for more at https://x.com/bcreativefirm.

About the Author

Hello, I'm Dave, the Creative Director at BABAZURI CREATIVE FIRM. Driven by a deep passion for creativity and entrepreneurship, I specialize in graphic design, digital writing, and much more. My interests span across art, design, open-source software, digital entrepreneurship, autos, psychology, and theology. I'm on a mission to make a meaningful impact as an internet entrepreneur, YouTuber, and eBook creator.

Read more at https://x.com/bcreativefirm.

BABAZURI Creative Firm

About the Publisher

Babazuri Creative Firm is a dynamic creative agency based in Nairobi, Kenya. We specialize in creating high-quality design resources, ebooks, and engaging YouTube video tutorials on using open-source software.

Our services also include graphic design, web design, logo design, digital writing, blogging, social media influencing, content creation, magazine design and editing, copywriting, filming, photography, and digital marketing.

Our dedicated team is passionate about bringing innovative and impactful ideas to life, helping businesses and individuals elevate their brands and achieve their creative goals.

Read more at https://bcreativefirm.co.ke.

www.ingramcontent.com/pod-product-compliance
Lightning Source LLC
LaVergne TN
LVHW090333210926
848480LV00004B/1396